How To Find A Husband

Carol Bellavance

authorHOUSE®

AuthorHouse™
1663 Liberty Drive, Suite 200
Bloomington, IN 47403
www.authorhouse.com
Phone: 1-800-839-8640

This book is a work of non-fiction. Unless otherwise noted, the author and the publisher make no explicit guarantees as to the accuracy of the information contained in this book and in some cases, names of people and places have been altered to protect their privacy.

© 2007 Carol Bellavance. All rights reserved.

No part of this book may be reproduced, stored in a retrieval system, or transmitted by any means without the written permission of the author.

First published by AuthorHouse 11/12/2007

ISBN: 978-1-4259-5508-3 (sc)

Printed in the United States of America
Bloomington, Indiana

This book is printed on acid-free paper.

Chapter 1

Catherine: Mom what is true love?

I learnt about the meaning of love when I was about your age by reading a book that I have kept ever since and that I still read at least once every year, just to reassure myself that I am still on the right track in the matter of love. From that book I have learnt that love is to desire, to choose and mostly it is to suffer, because of our need of absolution and perfection which will never be satisfied in this life. It is to depend on someone or something. It is to need his presence, his acceptation. It is also based on an interest as we can read in "Le Petit Prince" from the French author Antoine de St-Exupery, which is, by the way, the book I was telling you about:

In the book when the little prince explains to the roses seen in a garden why his rose is so special he says: "My rose, a passerby could think that she looks like you, but alone she is more important than all of you because it is her that I watered, it is her that I put under a globe, it is her that I protected from the wind, and it is from her that I removed the crawling millipedes. It is her alone I have listened to complain or brag or even at times to be silent. It is because she is my rose." The fox, his new friend who was listening added with philosophy: "It is the time that you lost for her that makes her so important to you." And that, my precious daughters, sums it up for me, because if you ever one day decide to read the book you will see that his beloved rose was not always a nice one, she was at times plain difficult, being terribly self-centered, yet he listened to her and he cared for her with so much love.

Love between a man and a woman, two individuals that are so similar and yet so different at the same time can be challenging. Yet, I believe that love can last a life time as long as there is an evolution in our approach. Like water, it must never stagnate to be alive and pure, it needs to be allowed to breathe. It is also a choice, an act of the will.

Love is based on responsibility: When we love, we become responsible of the spiritual, emotional and physical wellbeing of our loved one. In the Little Prince we can read the fox commenting to the little prince "You become responsible forever of what you tamed. You are responsible of your rose." It can be seen as a sense of duty too.

Respect is another important element and again in the Little Prince you can read: "It was only a fox similar to thousand others, but I made him my friend and now he is unique in the whole world." Respect means to accept someone as he is, without trying to change him in order to answer to our own conception of what he should be.

The last element necessary in order to love is the knowledge, and this is the most important of all because it is the key that will enable our love to last for a lifetime.

What do you know of his nature, of his reactions, of his character or of his requirements? If the choice of a boyfriend/husband is based solely on his physical aspect, it would be like when we go buying a car and we would base our choice uniquely on its appearance, model and color, as you can guess that is not a very smart thing to do. There is more than appearance in life in regard to things and beings.

That would leave out any information about the engine, maintenance requirements, gas/mileage, year of make (an older model might end up with more mechanical problems). While you can't really compare a man to a car, the principle is the same; you just don't look at a potential mate for his physical attributes. You can't be in love with someone just because he happens to be great looking, that would be infatuation and to be infatuated means to be deprived of sound judgment by acting like a fool. You may lust after him, but lust has nothing to do with love. Just imagine that you are looking for the perfect gown for prom night: You go from store to store until you find the one that you want. You try it and it is a perfect fit, immediately you know that you must have it because no other gown will do, that is the one that you have set your heart on.

Let's say, you buy it three months in advance, a couple of months later you are hunting stores for matching accessories and while walking down the sidewalk by the downtown store windows you see a prettier gown in the display window, now you walk home thinking what a fool you have been (and if only you had waited a little longer or had not insisted to have some minor adjustments done on it, now you can't bring it back) you are stuck with it! If you had waited you would have found this marvelous gown and you would be wearing it at the prom, becoming the envy of every girl going that night.

Now you are sad and feeling a little betrayed by that gown because it does not have the same shine anymore (at least in your eyes), the same can be said with your fiancé or husband. Once you are married, I can guarantee you that it is only a matter of time before you encounter a better version of what you have! So when this happens you will need to be disciplined enough to be content with what you have and view your husband as a precious gift from God and in time you will understand that the new man that you view as a better model will also with time wear out or you will start to find fault with him too! I have seen many people going through a divorce because of an affair and they all ended up with lots of regrets. I haven't seen any exceptions. Happiness is a choice!

The physiology of male and female:

Let's try to understand the nature of man and woman from the moment of conception. At the time of conception, the 23 chromosomes from the egg combine with the 23 chromosomes from the sperm to produce a zygote, or if you prefer a fertilized egg cell, which then combined has 46 chromosomes. Two of these chromosomes will determine the sex. The offspring always inherits an X chromosome from the mother. If the father also gives an X chromosome, the offspring will be female which reads XX. If the father gives a Y chromosome, then the offspring is male which reads XY. Even though a child's ultimate sex is determined at conception, an embryo doesn't start developing into a boy or girl until about after six weeks of pregnancy. If the child inherited a Y chromosome from his father, a gene on the Y called the SRY gene turns on. This gene is just like a master switch that turns on all the other genes necessary to become a boy. If this gene is not present, it is then that the embryo develops as a girl. That sounds very simple, but there are so many things that can go wrong in this process.

Even though the SRY turns on the other genes, if any of them are mutated (the result of taking a particular turn or just what we call an accident of nature), the full sexual phenotype may not develop. For example, the testosterone which is a male hormone, is responsible for beginning the development of male characteristics. If this gene is mutated or the gene for their cell receptors is mutated, male development won't begin and that means that the child will be born looking like a female when from the origin point it was meant to be a male. Many accidents from nature can happen at that developmental stage, if a XX pair breaks a part of the X, it could become a Y and now some scientists are starting to think that it may explain why a male may be attracted to other males in certain cases of homosexuality.

The psychology of love:

We also need to learn about the psychology of love: Each person needs some space. If a needy partner falls in love with an independent person that would bring trouble in the relationship as soon as the novelty of sex wears out. The independent partner might react negatively in what he will view as an invasion of his privacy by the clingy partner.

The way we relate to our partner through identification is also very important. Some men call their wife the same way that their children do, calling your wife "Mother or Mom" that is a sure way to kill love. For, such men are trying to find a maternal substitute through her. The same thing can happen to a woman the day her husband becomes a father, she will assimilate him to her own father, looking for a paternalistic relationship…by doing so, the inhibitions from their childhood can resurface and that will bring conflict between the spouses. Often, one is trying to find security through this identification. This can be explained by the fact that at the beginning the child lives in symbiosis with the mother. Then there is the weaning that brings on separation, and the regret that comes with it. Many men and women seem to be unable to pass that stage and they are the ones who will identify the spouse to the parent, all this, just to be able to feel safe again.

Chapter 2

Marie-Claire: What are the major differences between the masculine and the feminine psychology?

I can assure you that the rhythm is quite different. A woman is a being that starts her life in wait; by that, I mean, she waits for the man who will love her, who will turn her into a new person. She is also a being of worries that will be with her during the early and middle years. She will worry about her husband, about her children or about life itself. Finally, she will become a being animated by wisdom in the late years. Her wisdom will be the result of her experiences and observations from the past. She will be reflective and distant to help her focus better on the lessons she learnt.

Man is her opposite. He starts as a being detached, distant from the rest but not because he is reflecting on his past like the woman, but because he is preparing his future. He will become a being of worries too as time goes by, and then during the later years he will be in the wait, waiting for a presence and waiting for tender loving care. In her affectivity the woman expects tenderness from a man, the knowledge of a choice that makes her a new woman all over again, that distinguishes her from her peers and complements her. Of course maternity is the awakening of the heart and mind. The woman is at the service of the specie: she is conditioned by her reflexes.

While fecundity for a man lasts a moment, it will last a lifetime for a woman. Sexual freedom is only an illusion, when you actually think about it. Fear of pregnancy is normal. Especially if the woman has seen another woman had a difficult pregnancy or gave birth to a sick child or to a child with genetic problems; however if nothing is done about it, trouble in the marriage will result. For one thing her fears might cut off her desire toward her husband and in turn he will feel abandoned or rejected, not understanding her coldness.

* If you want a man to find you attractive you must embrace your feminine side. ~~The most~~ Don't underestimate the power of scent. A woman must smell good at all times...

* As a general rule men prefer their women curvy and round in all the right places.

* Flirt with your femininity!

CHAPTER 3

Gabrielle: What are the biggest differences between a man and a woman?

An American psychoanalyst known as Dr. Theodore Reik, who established psychoanalyze in the U.S.A., came to the discovery of the following differences between men and women that helped him during his 30 odd years of practice.

Man:

==Men want women to be simple, squared, reasonable and logic all the time...but very lady-like also.== As you can see these beings who pride themselves for their rational logic want cubes, but they want them to be round! A man is in reality a child who wants to play, his toy being his work. For him this is a very serious game, it will easily become the center of his existence. As a teen, men know nothing of women. But as the years go by, while they learn more about them, in the end they still know nothing of us.

Nature has not prepared a man to become a husband, much less a father, so he improvises. A hard working man does not let his mind falter in the direction of his woman; his thoughts are focused on what he does unless his attention weakens. In fact, he only wants the presence of his wife at certain moments. Most husbands are gentlemen, and as a result they never talk about their wife. Men want to stay the same with each coming day. The nicest thing a man likes to hear is: I am so proud of you. A man will try to avoid crying to not pass for a weakling. A married man often will envy his single friends. Love will make a man loose control for a few hours at the time. His attitude toward pleasure is simple, intense, entire and urgent. They have a strong sense of principles. A man can be proud or ashamed of his wife but you can be sure that it will never alter what he thinks of himself in any way. Man will talk about himself simply: he thinks that the woman is immediately impressed by whatever passion consumes him be it aeronautical engineering, bridge construction, hockey or football. For a man, the woman who listens to him with all her attention is a very intelligent woman. When they grow old many a man become unhappy, it's the result of loosing "his toy" or his work. Happiness for a man is quite a piece of work: He wants to gain a place in the world of his peers: Power and/or recognition. A man will abandon his freedom to love and to be enabled to love. A man gets married for three reasons: 1- To have a friend, an admirer and someone with whom he can exchange ideas. 2- To have sex readily and conveniently. 3- To have children, a continuity of himself through the future generation, a proof that he was essential at a point in time.

Woman:

A woman never fails to take the religion and the nationality of her husband as easily as she will take his name. We have a say in French that goes like "She who takes a man takes also the land!"

When something happens in a woman's life you can be sure that there is a man close by. A woman will observe a man. Upon waking to guess his humor, when he comes home to know how his day at work was. At the dinner table to know if he likes what she prepared to know if he still thinks of her. She is so curious about what he thinks of her at different moments of the day and evening (by the way that annoys men greatly because they want some privacy in their emotional life).

The woman may cook, clean the laundry, run errands or work, but is never far from her husband for he is constantly in her thoughts. Almost everything she does, she does in reference to him. The woman is a worried lover; she is a worried mother too. Her man made her go from childhood to motherhood. Now she is responsible for life.

That goes to show that women who want their equality to men have simply renounced to their superiority! Women can't stop celebrating the husband for he hold the greatest role in their lives. A woman always wishes for the presence of her husband at her sides. Out of love she wants to be with him. Every woman dreams of waking up a new woman every morning. The nicest thing a woman wants to hear is "I love you." Women try not to cry just to not look too ugly. A married woman feels sorry for her single friends. Love metamorphoses a woman for the rest of her life. The attitude of a woman toward love is emotional and slow to reach a paroxysm.

The woman's self-esteem depends on the kind of husband she chose to walk with through life. Women have a better sense of reality and have fewer principles than men.

To get a man interested, a woman wants to talk, but she learns quickly to keep quiet. First, because she fears to appear inferior to him and secondly because to listen to a man it is to seduce him and every woman knows that much.

Old women are at peace because they kept the essential: a house and grand-children. Women want happiness and they know that this can be achieved by conquest only: The conquest of a man's heart and to keep his heart to herself as long as she can.

Every woman cries. Some of them cry more than others, while some will cry louder than others, some cry with more reasons than others, but in the end they all cry simply because a woman is a tangle of emotions.

Women marry for three major reasons: 1- To have a man to herself to cherish. 2- To receive affection and to get security in sexual relations. 3- To receive proof of love, often done through the usual gifts a husband will bring to her: flowers, jewels, chocolates and perfumes.

A superficial exchange in the couple will not be enough. We need to find time for a real conversation. Don't try to joke your way out of it or buried yourself into a TV show or a book when things don't go your way. Misunderstandings arise often from the way we express our feelings. There are three personalities in each one of us: For the woman, there is the mother, the adult and the child. For the man there is the father, the adult and the child. If asked an adult question the person answers with an adult answer that is not a problem, but if the adult answers the same question as a child or a mother, that is when the fighting will begin. It is necessary that both adults answer and ask as adults and not as children or parents. Another aspect of communication that is often neglected is the punctuation. It is not what we say that hurts the other as much as how we say it. It is not easy to communicate with another person; we need to focus on the other instead of wasting energy on ways to prove that we are right all the while pretending that we are listening. And while on the subject, an important thing to remember is that adults too can get "grumpy" when tired, especially after a long day at work, never ever start an important discussion once the sun has gone down, make it a rule to never approach an important issue late at night and I guarantee you that this little trick will protect you from many heated discussions and major heartbreak in your marital life!

Chapter 4

Catherine: What should I look for in a man?

Is there a great difference of ages between the two of you? That could bring some psychological problems with the child or complications between the spouses as he was educated in a different era. My girlfriend Luisa got married with a man 12 years older than her. While Dominic her husband is a great companion and friend, Luisa found that 25 years later in the marriage, Dominic's energy level was much lower than the energy.

Luisa still had to go out and travel. He would tire easily and he rather spends the weekends at home sitting in front of the TV while Luisa wanted to go out, visit friends and travel. During the children rearing years Luisa also noted that Dominic had less patience than her also his life conceptions were at times very different than hers, having been raised himself in a different époque.

Is he in good health? What about his genetic background? This is an important factor to consider if you want to stay home while the children are growing. Take my friend Mona who is married to George, a quadriplegic and they led a very happy life together. Because Mona had been severely abused physically by a violent father while growing up, she had vowed that no man would ever lift his hands on her and by searching for someone who would treat her right and not someone who could hurt her physically, she knew from the beginning that only a physically handicapped man could make her feel safe. So when she met George at the age of 17, she decided that he was the one for her.

They raised two beautiful children and are still happily married 30 years later! Mona was in good health and worked as an interior decorator while George has worked as a psycho-therapist for teens with difficulties.

Is he really intelligent? I am not talking of his education, how eloquent he is or of his achievements in the work place. I am talking of how he reacts toward you. Can he talk without getting annoyed with you if your opinions differ from his? Does he accept to be shown his errors without becoming defensive and putting the blame on everything and everyone else? Does he accept advices well? Does he give you a chance to disagree with him without accusing you or putting you at fault? Can he listen without interrupting you? If you have answered yes to those questions that means that he possesses real intelligence that he knows and accepts his limitations and is willing to learn from the experience of someone else.

Is he well-balanced? Does he suffer from any mental illness such as bipolar disorder or schizophrenia? These are serious illnesses and the atmosphere at home could be jeopardized by his instability. While in many cases medication will help, remember that it is not going to cure him and totally protect him from mood swings, depression and other manifestation of his specific illness. If you have children together it will be harder but not impossible, the real question is: are you ready and willing to embark in a journey that you know will be tough and are you ready to commit yourself no matter how hard it will get? Are you willing to follow a diet and/or a routine for the rest of your life if necessary? It takes faith and strength of the heart to love all the way.

Is he loyal? If you realized that during your days of courtship he cheated on you, chances are pretty good that he will continue to do so once the novelty of marriage with you wear off. If this is the case: break the relationship now. He has either no self discipline or is not ready to commit himself exclusively to you.

Does he have an optimistic view of life? Hardship will not lack during the years ahead, so if he is easily depressed or has a pessimistic view of the world around him this will bring sufferance on the rest of the family. How will he react if you both lose a child through illness or accident? Will he be there to support you or will he retrieve to a private world leaving you to fend for yourself emotionally? What if one of you becomes sick or handicapped? What if he looses his work and can't find anything else for over a year? What if a child is born with mental retardation? Is he going to put the blame on you for it?

The stress of such an event is enough to shatter a marriage once the blaming game starts, and if no one is blaming anyone, what if you feel guilty about it, if you take it as a personal failure to produce a healthy child for your husband? When bad things happens, and yes there will be unfortunate events happening during the course of your life, to sail through you will need a man who is emotionally strong, who has a good sense of humor but most of all, a man who is fully committed to you.

Our lives can be compared to a big wheel, when it goes up, we are feeling on top of the world, but when it goes down, that is when we need to reach out for help. The good news is that life goes on, the good, like the bad will come to pass, there is a time for everything, but when you navigate through a bad storm, believe me, you will need to get your strength from somewhere or someone. So be prepared and plan in advance for those hard days ahead of you.

Now to use a popular question in the work force: What does teamwork mean to him? Can he compromise? If he rather work alone and does not collaborate well with others, chances are that sharing with you his feelings will not be happening, you may end up feeling rather lonely, a man who does not share his feelings may at first appear like a strong rock that is good to lean on. I have seen many women fall for such men (mostly relater types, very talkative extroverts), and due to the immense complexity of the human personalities I cannot generalize, as I am sure there are exceptions, but just know that many men will be unable or unwilling to share their feelings. I have observed that the more a woman is a people relater (talkative person) the more she is particularly drawn to that kind of man. Remember that in 10-15 years from now, when you will feel the need to talk and to confide in him and hear his confidence: this man will not change. He will still be the introvert, the strong rock that you felt love with, he will not be comfortable to share his feelings with you, some introverts have an emotional structure that simply prevent them from understanding another being, especially from the opposite sex, now and in the years to come. They just clam up (in some cases it is done in order to avoid conflict, especially if as a child he was never taught how to deal with conflict or has bad memories or had a childhood in a house where conflicts were constant). Surely you heard the old song by Paul Simon that is sometimes played on the "Oldies" radio station. It is called "I am a Rock." Rocks feel no pain but risk to give you pain in the long run!

Some men won't take any responsibilities their words or actions and always blame the others for what goes wrong in his life you can be assured that you will be blamed for whatever goes wrong in the marriage. There are no magic wands that can change people.

Is he a big spender? Don't let yourself be fooled by the gifts he is offering you while dating. While they could be the result of his love for you and they could be provided through sacrifice, it is possible that he just does not has any financial sense and that could means that you will be living in debts most of your married life. While on the subject, there have been many debates on whether women should be working or simply stay home to raise the family. I would say that there are advantages and disadvantages to both choices. Just ensure that whatever you decide, you are not going to be financially dependent of a man. If you choose to stay home, ascertain yourselves that you have a circle of friends to surround and support you, so that you do not become totally isolated and lonely as if this should happen, you would naturally tend to turn toward the husband to talk all of your frustrations and that would put too much pressure on your relationship with the tired husband who will be assaulted by the need to talk of his wife.

Remember, men return home often deflated of energy and what they need the most is tranquility and the safety of a cozy home, not more verbal noise or a house in disarray.

Is he from the same social or cultural background as you? While you may think that it does not matter because you are not marrying his family, you will share your children that are issued from their bloodline and you can be assured that the in-laws will want to participate in the education of their grand-children. In fact, his family after investing so many years in the education of their son, will most likely want to share in his new life. In some matriarchal cultures the mother-in-law is the one who rules on the rest of the family and until you in turn become a mother-in-law yourself you will have no say in the family decisions! In patriarchal cultures the father is the head figure of a family.

That means that as the son of that family, your new husband might be called often to his parent's house to help with the process of decision making.

Are you aware of all his faults? Are you comfortable with them? Is he a jealous man? Someone who risks controlling your every move? It could be that he has a very low self-esteem and that would not be good for your relationship. Is he selfish? In this world you find two kinds of people: one is a giver while the other one is a taker. If you are both givers, it will be great. If you are a taker married with a giver again you should have a great marriage. But if both of you are takers, your life together will become a living hell for the both of you!

When I decided to marry your dad I knew right from the beginning that I would never become rich and that I would never own a house or have nice diamonds but since I am not much of a materialist, it did not matter then and it certainly does not matter now, but it is not for every one to be spending a life flat broke! In truth the basic needs are not costly, but the society in which we live tries very hard to create wants that may be interpreted as needs. It is for you to be smart enough to make the difference between if what you want is truly what you need.

Is he a gambler? Does he dabble into pornography? What about drugs or alcohol? If that is the case chances are very slim that he will ever change. So think hard about that. These addictions are serious and will destroy any chances of happiness in your marriage.

Don't let him minimize such a problem. People get trapped into addictions and while I some seem able to walk away from it while others can't, (maybe it has to do with strength of character) be warned, many couples have separated due to that enslavement. Recently

I was reading an article where children as young as eight years old show signs of addiction to video games and computers, there are even food and sex addictions among teens, and in most cases the parents did not know about their children's addictions, so I think that addictions might be more prevalent in our modern society that we realize.

Your grand-father battled addictions all his life with pornography and alcohol, it wrecked his first marriage to your grand-mother, and his second marriage was not easy, for his second wife admitted to me how hard it had been on her and that if she had had a trade or a profession, she would not have stayed married to him, but without financial independence she felt that she was trapped and had to endure the marriage.

Eventually, he lost his work and his reputation due to these addictions when he was re-called in Montreal by his company.

Also, many girls between the ages of 17-20 seem to have such unrealistic expectations of marriage, the one thing that surprise me the most when I left my province was how Western-Canadian and American girls were buying into romantic ideas more readily when compared to the Québécoises. I believe that it is due to the many "chick flick movies" their expectations of the prince charming entering their lives is real to them, so please bring your expectation down to a healthy level of reality. Even princesses don't live happily ever after; we all saw what happened to the British Royal couple: Charles and Diana and also with Princess Caroline of Monaco, their divorces made the headlines!

Leave those fantasies with Hollywood. And please never go out with a man for his car or money or even status, these things can be lost or taken away, what will happen then?

Does he come from a family that has the two parents? Or is he from a single parent family? Let's skip political correctness here, political correctness, while it has its usefulness in public relations, here it would only serve to mask the facts behind the scenes. If he was brought up by his mother, ask where was the father? Who is the man who took his place? Where did he get his role model? This is crucial, for nowadays we see many single mothers trying to raise sons and that is a recipe for disaster. No woman, no matter how high and noble her intentions are, can teach a boy to become a man. You cannot teach what you are not or pass along knowledge that you do not possess. In some instances the love that the woman should have showered on the husband is showered on the son and that could bring a fixation of the son on the mother and what the mother wants…the mother will get, regardless of your idea on the subject. Be warned. If he did not grow up under the care of a grand-father or uncle who lived in the same house provide the uncle is not a teen himself. Otherwise risk is high that this man will have something lacking during the formation of his character. Recently I was talking to a woman who was telling me that her 16 year old son was the role-model for her two year old grand-son that lived with her. Now, how on earth is it possible that a child could be mistaken for a man? I know of no 16 year old boys who can act like a man! In many instances a single mother does not have the necessary strength to raise a boy, her energy will be spent at work and with the house chores, she will have no patience left when she gets home and will either be on the son's case every minute, which will alienate him, or she will just give up and let him have it his own way, which means there will be no parental guidance or surveillance of the teenager's activities. In either case that result in a young man who has no discipline, no self control, no respect; and without a father role model his chances to behave toward you the way a man should are very slim.

Who are his friends, other boys that did not get both parents like him? Take Dirk: He was left in Montreal at age 15 by his father who was working on a contract in Guinea, the one left in charge was his 20 year old step-brother who certainly did not have enough maturity to take care of four siblings/step-siblings. Dirk, your father, was lucky, he made good friends at school and was supervised by the parents of one of his friends quite closely. Unfortunately it was not the case for the others who turned out to have great difficulties in their personal relationships (divorce, out of wedlock birth, alcoholism).

Are you proud of him? Are you looking forward to introduce him to your friends and family? If that is not the case, then it is a clear indication that something like an important value or trait of character is lacking. Maybe his background is too different or you perceive that something is not right. Is it the way he wears his clothes? Or the way that he talks or moves, let it be a strong warning, as once you are married there will be no way to change him. Basically you are getting him "as is". In other words, what you see is what you get!

What do you have in common? You will share a house together, that means you better have similar views in decoration and food. The first year of my marriage with my husband, we lived in Africa and although my parents had warned me, especially that he is from another nationality. My father told me that the Dutch men he had met in his life had a tendency to be strongly opinioned in regard to decorations of their houses and it was one of those warnings that I did not pay attention to, thinking "Ah once we are married I will change his taste." WRONG! It was a very difficult first year. While I am certain that not all Dutch men are like that my Dutch husband was like that!

In the end I decided to let him do according to his taste, since I was loosing the battle of will, and after thinking it over I decided that in 10 years or so, maybe I could get my own way to decorate. Well I can tell you that today, some 23 years later he still has a very

How To Find A Husband

determined mind when it comes to home décor. There is a say about Dutch people that goes something like this "Wooden shoes, wooden head, wouldn't listen…"

Fortunately this is a difference that I can live with, but is it one that you could?

Since we all are different as far as personalities and tastes go you need to ascertain yourself of what are the things that you can accept and live with and what are the things that you will not compromise with.

And while some activities will hold you together, such as with your father and I, we both love to travel, try new food and to meet with people of different cultures. Others will separate you. You just need to find the right balance for a healthy couple life.

For a while the traveling we did was fine, but eventually we changed, one cannot be eternally on the road in search of adventures. After a few years you will need something that will help you to stay connected. It could be a shared interest in gardening; collecting something together (stamps, antiquities, etc ;) hiking, camping, writing, dancing, cinema, photography. You will need also something that is different such as an occupation or activity that is your own, it could be photography, sewing, drawing. In my marriage we both love science-fiction movies and to experience exotic food and dancing.

Your father loves gardening; many hours are spent inside his green house when he comes home after a long day at work. His other hobby is about wine making, where he joined a club for wine artisans. I for one love writing so that is what I do when alone and reading and learning new things.

Chapter 5

Marie-Claire: So you married dad and were not even in love with him?

That is right Marie-Claire; I was not in love with him. But I knew that he was a good man and that in time love would come if I gave it a chance. Remember daughter: love is not a feeling, if your marriage is to work out you need to know who you are marrying and most of all why you are marrying. I married my best friend because I want to share my life with him!

Do you have the same religion or philosophical beliefs? Our core personality comes from our spiritual belief, the sum of the teachings we received since our earliest childhood experiences. If you do not share the same religious belief there will be an association of your two personalities but no real union. We cannot run away from who we are and even if one of you should change your religion to be closer or more unify to your spouse you will be years behind in knowledge from the partner who spent some 20 years studying and learning about his spiritual belief. That is why when the children arrive if you belong to different faiths; ask who will teach them and which faith will they belong to? Now remember that as a Catholic you will be requested to have the children rose into our faith if you marry someone belonging to another denomination. But if you think about it: You cannot just sit back and say that once they are old enough they will choose their belief system. For the same reason that you would not just sit there and wait that they grow up before you teach them how to talk under the pretense that they will want to choose their own language to communicate. You would deprive the child from important learning and that child would invariably become retarded if you do not start right away to communicate with him. It is the same thing with religion; you have the responsibility for his/her soul and cannot just sit back and disengage yourself from your parental responsibilities toward them. Spiritual immaturity is a real challenge for the partner who is more knowledgeable, it is not sufficient to have the same religion nowadays, but through prayers alone and together it can be overcome as long a the most immature partner gets some form of weekly exposure with groups from their church.

How about children? Do you want some? What if one of you is barren? Would you adopt? In the event, that you can produce your own children. How will you space their arrivals? These are important issues that need to be addressed before marriage. It takes money and a good health to raise children and it is our duty as parent to not bring to this world more children that we can afford to provide with the bare necessities to succeed in life such as proper clothing, a roof over their heads, nutritious food and a good education that will enable them to be proud citizens, able to contribute for something to the society where they choose to live.

Meet the parents! Look at his father closely for there are many chances that he will look and act just like his old man in 10 or 15 years from now…after all, his father was his role model. Does he appear well-disciplined? Does he seem sincere? How does he treats his wife? Does he appear too authoritarian or is he being dominated by his wife?

Make a list of what you want out of marriage and ask your fiancé to do the same and discuss openly. Last but not least, if there is any secret that you have and are not proud of, maybe you want to bring it now to him, because no matter how careful you were at concealing from your family it is only a matter of time before he finds out…Robby had a secret he never told Lisa: that while engaged to her, he slept with her cousin Lydia, he called it a one night stand, the result of too much drinking in a bar where he met her by chance and had made Lydia swore to secrecy so that Lisa would never find out…well, 20 years later Lisa found out…they are now divorced. In the case of Jenny it was different: she had experienced with her room-mate at university, she just wanted to know how it felt to have sex with another woman, well one night 12 years later Jenny and Tony came face to face with the room-mate who had just arrive to town as the new family doctor and since Tony was a doctor…another divorce! If you can't bring yourself to tell him write to him a letter but please do not keep such a secret to yourself as when he finds out he will feel betrayed by you, the one he trusted. If you fear break up it is better that it ends now than later when the children are there!

Chapter 6

Marie-Claire: Why do people divorce? Is it because of secrets that are found out?

No, not always. There are four main reasons that couples will fight.

Money: We all need it, but sometimes due to inexperience one may tend to overspend it while the partner may want to accumulate it, it has to do a lot with the family where you grew up. If money was tight and you heard your parents argue a lot about it, then you may become insecure in the matters of money and they only peace you fill find will be by hording it into the bank and live very carefully with what you allow yourself to use for living expenses. On the other hand your partner may have grown up in a house where there were plenty of it and as a result will tend to be careless with it and view it as a tool to get what he wants. Both of you should be apt to participate to the household budget and make a list of what is acceptable for each one. So, you know where to stand from the beginning. Take a class together at college or a seminar on financial planning.

The in-laws: In many cases men have more difficulties to leave their mother and father to take a wife and start a new life. My father, lived just a mile away from his parents and was there every day for an hour or so, and what his parents decided my mother had to abide by it. Their word was the law and there was nothing she could do or say that could change it. She admitted spending the majority of her married life angry at him and at his family but in her days there was little a woman could do. She felt tricked by her husband and trapped by her in-laws who would drop by uninvited and take the liberty to rearrange her kitchen and cupboards, even her wardrobe would be regularly visited to check if she was not making their son and brother spend too much on herself. Living on a farm she did not have anywhere to go and without education there was no work outside the farm for her.

Sex: Does he want it all the time? He never seems to get enough, to the point it is bothersome to you? He may be high drive. Or does he just want it on Saturdays? Are you always the one to initiate it? You find that there is no place for any spontaneity in your marriage; everything must be scheduled in advance? Because he never takes the first steps to seduce you, you feel that he is just not interested in you anymore, well, let me assure you that

How To Find A Husband

it does not means that he does not love you, it could be just the way he is personality wise. In fact you are pretty confident that there would be no sex if you did not ask for it…He may be working in a field where paying attention to detail is vital, like an accountant, financial planner, I have notice over the years that many women married to such men felt that they were not loved or stimulated by their husbands who had no imagination when it came to intimacy with their partner, now it is not to say that every man or woman working in the field of finances lack imagination and make poor sex partners. (In fact some men and women belonging to other fields also feel happy only with advanced planification), but I met Lucy who was married to Glenn a financial controller and Glenn seemed to need to plan even the most intimate moment with his wife using a weekly calendar to enter the time and day that he wanted sexual intercourse with his wife. He loved her and felt insecure if a time was not entered for it in his daily planner. This may seem funny to you but I have seen some couples with that exigency.

In the case of Lucy and Glenn that brought on a divorce even when Lucy understood that it was just the way that Glenn was, he did not like surprises in his life. It is most unfortunate that this was not talked about and discovered until marriage had been consumed…It was a painful divorce for both of them as they cared deeply for one another but alas not with enough maturity or wisdom to accept one another and view their marriage as a precious gift from God, the other's personality and needs. This is an important part of your life and that needs to be discuss prior commitment. You don't see the fun in having sex because you never have experienced an orgasm? Or you stopped since the birth of your first child? (I heard many times by women who gave birth to daughters that they stopped having orgasms once they resume their sexual activities and what they all had in common: was to have had sex before marriage with men). In any case, whatever the problem is I would urge you to have a complete pre-nuptial checkup done by a gynecologist just to be informed of any problems. I knew a girl who went to see a doctor for a medical examination and it was discovered that she was born without a clitoris and was told that she could never experience an orgasm, so she decided that marriage was not for her and joined a religious order where she further her studies got a degree, traveled extensively throughout the African Continent and today says that is considers herself as a very happy woman, she is now in her 60s and teaches at a nice located university. On the other hand I met Mary who is an artist, and who was told the same thing by her gynecologist some 25 years ago, and she decided to marry and today has two children and a husband that she loves very much and led a very nice life exposing her art and selling it throughout North America. My advice for you would be to follow the Biblical Principles of Marriage found in 1Corinthians 7: 3, 4, 5: "Let the husband render to his wife the affection due to her, and likewise also the wife to the husband. The wife does not have authority over her own body, but the husband does.

And likewise the husband does not have authority over his own body, but the wife does." When this is understood by the couple that should provide happiness. Now while it is normal for man to want it more than woman, it is because they are made differently than us, they complement us, so you are totally normal to not want it as much as him. Imagine if both want it all the time nothing would get done on this planet! Respect one another and this respect will be achieved through dialogue before you tie the knot.

Children: We tend to want to raise them the way we were ourselves raised. After all we can only teach what we know and what we know we learnt from our parents. If you come from a strict family, chances are you will want your children follow clearly defined rules from day one, and if your partner comes from a family where there were no rules, chances he will not want to make up some. He will say something along the lines:

"I grew up just fine without them and our children will too." For one thing he would not know where to start and where to put boundaries! So disagreement will be arising. In any case always bear in mind that while you and your husband made the physical children it is God who made their souls. Be gentle with them.

Although I do not have the perfect recipe to prevent disagreements from arising.

Just be aware of it and you can always ask the opinions of your older friends or relatives who have older children.

Chapter 7

Gabrielle: I don't know mom, because the Bible say to women to submit to their husbands and I do not think that is fair or even right.

Actually it is a fair commend for if you read correctly in Ephesians 5:22, 23. It says: "Wives submit to your own husbands, as to the Lord. For the husband is head of the wife, as also Christ is head of the Church; and He is the Savior of the body. Therefore like the Church is submitted to Christ, so let the wives be to their own husbands in everything." And if you read further in Ephesians5:25, 28 It says:" Husbands, love your wives just as Christ also loved the Church and gave Himself for it. So husbands ought to love their own wives as their own bodies; he who loves his wife loves himself." I think that the implication is great here. The woman is submitting to her husband only in the measure that he is submitting to Christ. So basically your marriage is like a love triangle, where there you are in one corner your husband in the other and God in the upper one.

Unfortunately today instead of God we find, money, or careers, or even someone else. If your husband is not submitting to the Lord then there is no real union there, if your husband hurts you or the children, he is not submitting to Christ and therefore you have no rights to submit to him as by doing so you are not in line with God's teachings. You have a duty to protect yourself and your children.

Chapter 8

Catherine: What if I fall in love with someone else for a good reason while I am married?

Because true love is an act of the will in the same sense that happiness can be found only in the sense of a duty well accomplished many young couples make the tragic mistake to think that love is a feeling...Of course you will meet men that are more handsome, richer or more intelligent than the one you have! Don't give in, run away from temptation, regular daily prayers will help you but when it comes to sexual attraction, lust; run for your life, this seems to be a stronghold that Satan has in our lives. And there is no reason that is good enough to break a marriage contract through adultery. So, he can't satisfy you anymore sexually speaking, think hard because sex is a privilege not a right. You think he does not understand you; maybe it is true if you have not talked to him and I mean really opened your heart to him. Do whatever it takes to maintain your integrity and dignity, and it might mean walking over your heart, even your job. There is not a single reason good enough to start an affair with another man. Learn to draw from your spiritual resources. Also through the Bible study you will learn that contrary to a popular belief that love means to never have to say you are sorry. It is a myth, love demands that you say that you are sorry, you must learn to admit that you were wrong and asked your spouse for forgiveness. These are not easy words but then there are no easy marriage either!

1 Corinthians 13:4-7 has the perfect definition of what love is: "Love is patient, love is kind. It does not envy, it does not boast, it is not proud. It is not rude, it is not self-seeking, it is not easily angered, and it keeps no record of wrongs. Love does not delight in evil but rejoices with the truth. It always protects, always trusts, always hopes, and always perseveres." Replace the word love by your own name when you read this and you will see the difference it makes:

Love is patient can be replaced by Catherine is patient and that means Catherine is calm and self-restrained from punishing others either physically or emotionally for a wrong or for mistakes made. She is always forgiving.

Love is always kind can be read as Marie-Claire is always kind and that means that Marie-Claire's goodness of heart is expressed in actions for another's benefit.

Love does not envy can be read as Gabrielle does not envy and it means that Gabrielle is not being resentfully desirous of another's advantages, possessions or gifts. Not desirous of another's good that she does not or cannot have.

Love does not boast and is not proud, can be read as Catherine does not boast and she is not proud, it means that Catherine does not seek to be exalted by bragging around. She is not puffed up with pride and self-importance over nothing.

Love is not self-seeking can be read as Marie-Claire is not self-seeking and it means Marie-Claire does not insist on having her own way or rights. She looks out for the interest of others.

Love is not easily angered can be replaced by Gabrielle is not easily angered and it means Gabrielle never easily stirred to anger; never touchy or quick tempered.

Love keeps no record of wrongs can be replaced by Catherine keeps no record of wrongs. And that means Catherine bears a wrong without holding it against the one who has committed it. Never holds grudges; maintains a forgiving spirit; keeps no records of wrongs.

Love does not delight in evil could be read as Marie-Claire does not delight in evil means she views sin as God does. She is never glad over someone else's mistakes or sins.

Love always protects, always trusts and always hopes and always preserves could be read as Gabrielle always protects, always trusts always hopes and always preserves and it means Gabrielle endures any hardship for another's good. She is willing to help to carry another's burdens.

She would think the best of other people for Christ's sake. She would give others the benefit of the doubt. She would hold fast to God's promises. Hopes for the best for others and lastly she would stand courageously through any trial or hardship with patience and a thankful spirit for the sake of Christ and others.

Chapter 9

Catherine: What about homosexuals & marriage?

As the Biblical law states, it is very important to treat homosexuals the same way as we treat heterosexuals. They deserve the very same respect and consideration, while in some case it is the result of poor parenting or trauma from bad experiences, in many cases this is from birth, remember at the beginning when I told you that if a chromosome XX pair would suffer some kind of accident and break a part it could be read as XY. While this has never been proven, I remember asking about this to my biology teacher and although he hold a PH. D. he could not come with a satisfying answer; all he said to me was that it was plausible. Now as to whether homosexuals should be able to marry the answer is no. There is nothing wrong with our tendencies, feelings and tastes but the way we act upon them could be wrong or right. For example anger per se is never wrong or right, it is what I will do with it that will make the difference. If out of anger I denounce abuse, it is right but if out of anger I beat someone up or destroy a life, that is wrong. God says it is wrong and therefore it is so. He has his reasons just to name one that would bring social destabilization and it could also throw negative impressions on children that need guidance from both parents (I mean parents of opposite sex) to grow normally. Now to be heterosexual means that a person is attracted to the opposite sex, there is nothing wrong with it. But take a heterosexual person who sleeps around that is plain wrong. Again that only contributes to destabilize society.

Chapter 10

Marie-Claire: That is not fair, what about love for them?

There are plenty of things in this world that are not fair. When you were born the doctor thought you may had cerebral palsy, you were deprived of oxygen and your APGAR scoring was 2 out of 10. I consider it a miracle that you do not have it, but think about all those babies who are born with it or to those who are born missing a limb. Is that fair?

Of course not, but why do you expect life to be fair? I have a cousin, her name is Marie she is my age and lives on the East Coast; she told me that she's always been attracted to women for as long as she can remember and yet she made the choice to follow God's Command and has married and is still married with the same man and together they share two beautiful children, they have a good life in a nice town, and she is happy, she said she will never know the "thrill of having sex with another woman" but all things considered she is happy. She told me that she views it as "bearing her cross for the Lord" and nowadays she feels that she would have deprived herself of a beautiful family if she had followed her desires. She had to quit her job as a beautician as she felt the temptation too strong when working so closely on other women, and so she change fields completely she works in a nursery as she love to do floral arrangements for the customers, she is a real artist and all she did was to transfer her skills in art and she still creates beautiful artwork for weddings, etc.

Chapter 11

Gabrielle: So they cannot fall in love?

First of all I never really liked the word "fall" when talking about love it should be referred to as to grow in love since love is based on knowledge and not on feelings alone as I explained to you earlier. And remember feelings can be controlled while there is no wrong or right feelings, it would be wrong to give free reign to our passions, it soon would be chaos if everyone was doing as please. We are humans and we can subjugate our passions and harness that energy to accomplish something to be proud of with our lives. Look at art work some artists never married or even had a sexual life yet their creation is a result of deep felt love. We need to lead our lives with dignity. It means we need to work on our relationships in a godly way by centering our actions for the wellbeing of the others.

Chapter 12

Catherine: What about those of my classmates and friends who just moved in with their boy-friends surely it is not like adultery if they intend to eventually get married?

You mean trial marriages? Like in shacking up together for a few months or years? Studies have shown that these unions rarely work once they marry. This is what I call a natural union, a natural union is unholy. That means that God is not part of the equation. Marriage sanctifies sex; we refer to it as holy matrimony because marriage is a sacred Covenant that cannot be broken. Now let's not confuse it with a marriage annulment which can be decreed only when there was no real marriage for example in the case where a girl would be coerced into marrying a certain young man because she is pregnant. Or in the case where one of the two people who went through the ceremony is refusing to engage in sexual relationships or in the case that one of the two newly weds were not mature enough for instance when one did not disclose important personal information or having married for the money of the other one or for his/her status. After a lengthy investigation those by the Church then an annulment would be decreed.

Now to come back to living together without the grace of God that is risky business. One of the two does not want commitment, fearing obligations, unfortunately it deprives the woman from the much needed emotional stability, where is the love you can ask yourself? I once heard a cousin of mine who had just moved in with his new girl-friend say "Why should I pay for the milk when I can get the cow for free?" For me that comment did it; I promised myself that no man would ever say such an awful thing about me, today 25 years later I still feel bad for this poor lady. Sadly enough he was not the last one that I heard talking that way. Then I had a girl-friend Mariette, she moved in with Mr. Right but confided sadly that it was because he did not want to get married and because she loved him so much she felt compelled to trade her integrity and pretend that she was happy, the union lasted a few years then they had a civil marriage performed but that marriage became full of sadness and resentment; eventually he started to abuse her and having no where to turn, feeling ashamed she became very depressed and cut ties with the rest of us…the last I heard was that they were separated.

But you, my daughters, just think about the following: what are the real reasons behind such behavior? Your worth the love and the commitment of a good man, you are too precious in the eyes of God to settle for anything that risks to damage you spiritually and psychologically. So please do not give in to such a proposal from a fiancé. We are living in a culture where adultery is glamorized. Surveys show that the majority of people view this is a wrong thing to do but no one wants to take a stand and speak up against what they see and I suspect that the reason is that many have fallen into the same trap and feel foolish to speak against something they have tried themselves, shame and guilt would keep these poor souls quiet. The bottom line is if a young man refuses to marry you and want to try you first…he is not worth to be with you. Many young ladies have fallen for the "let's move in together" and have dearly regretted their move. Unfortunately we are proud beings and we certainly do not want to loose face or be "dumped" so we get ourselves into those precarious situations but I can promise you that no one comes out unscathed from their misadventure.

Chapter 13

Marie-Claire: Is sex as fun as it looks like to be from the movies that I've seen?

Well, as you know by now, the man and the woman are made different in regard to enjoying good sex. While for the man his pleasure is very intense and physical, for the woman it is more emotional. For example, while a man will find enjoyment on a minute notice, if the husband was in a bad mood earlier that day, I can guarantee you that unless he comes with a small present as a token of his love (or a peace offering if you prefer) the wife is not going to feel much of an orgasm! We are creatures of emotions and because we are emotional the answer is yes we can enjoy sex greatly but only when there is love between the two. For a woman to have an orgasm and enjoy it, she needs to feel safe, loved and cherished, she needs to feel wanted and needed by her man.

Only then can it be as fun as in the movies! But just bear in mind that if a woman could have the same physical orgasm as a man and as often as she wanted, nothing would get done. I mean everyone would be having sex all the time, everywhere couples would be at it and there would be no time for construction, cooking, working or anything else.

That goes to show that men and women were created to complete each other, so do not expect to get an orgasm each time you have sex if your husband has not prepare the mood first. Also I have heard over the years from many women who had had sex before marriage once they gave birth to a daughter for some reasons they became frigid, yet they were fine when they had sons but things started to change for them the moment they hold that tiny girl in heir arms. Obviously some psychological damage was created by their past behavior. This is not a statement that they would admit to their husbands, but that is an element that creates a diminution and a tension with their sexual life in the course of their marriage. Now girls it is getting late, it is time to go to bed.

Chapter 14

Catherine: But Mom there is still something that we haven't discussed. What if I am married and don't want any children, at least not right away?

Well while the child should the expression of love the reality of it is quite different. Fear of pregnancy can ruined intimacy between a couple, no doubt. For years the humans have let their impulsions guide them and heave lost the sense of what sex is all about and as a result do not understand anymore the importance of bringing children to the world.

A child is the expression of completion for a couple. It completes their state and celebrates their lives through completeness and assured meaning to their future or a sort of genetic memory, their lives become eternal through the following generations.

If a couple remains childless unless a good reason it will be a triple fault:

First toward ourselves as the child will drive us to give the best of ourselves and put all of our selfishness away.

Second toward the society as we have the duty to bring certain stability and to produce good citizens who will bring knowledge or ways to help their fellow humans through inventions or interventions that will help people.

Third toward God who gave us the comment to grow and multiply, to become co-creators with Him. Now if not having children is bad unless a good reason to have too many is also not good for three reasons.

It is an injustice toward the mother; it is not fair to have a new baby in your arms day in and day out, this pose a health risk as well if not physically then mentally and spiritually. It is also unfair toward the husband who will need to spread himself thin to educate his children and add to his worries about finances. Family time is very important and if the father does not have a good education to provide for a large family it will require that he gets a second and a third job to meet the needs of his family.

It is wrong to impose a new child to the existing siblings if it means to reduce the time shared together due to obligations toward the new born and toward careers or second income that has become a necessity in our time and age.

If we cannot assure the care of the child I do not believe that we have the right to bring that child into the world, it is not for the social welfare to assume the responsibility of the new lives introduced by irresponsible parents. Human procreation is not an animal act, it demands care and education, an education that will bring better conditions of life for the person its society and by extension the whole planet. It is not like the past century anymore where people lived together as families and lived out of their labor on the land.

Too many children in a family who does not have the income to assure their independence and education will bring a heavy load on the parents, siblings and ultimately on the society where they live.

Chapter 15

Marie-Claire: What must we choose then?

As an enlighten adult you will choose according the health and the ability to educate your children, granted every one is not destined to have a university degree, but every one should be able to master some kind of technique or trade that will lead to earn a good income in order to provide some service or knowledge to the society where you choose to live. It is good for your own pride too to be of some use to others.

Also we need to take into account the level of income of the parents and most of all the spiritual level of knowledge of the parents. While procreation is an act between man and woman it is also through God that the soul is conceived. That means a child that is not wanted or respected as a person but treated as a commodity to better the finances of the parents is a terrible thing. This has happened a few times in Quebec where the government was giving a monetary incentive to women who choose to have more children. Some immature women have gotten themselves pregnant for the $3,000.00 that they were hoping to receive from the government, for their personal benefit.

Chapter 16

Gabrielle: Can the woman choose or is it the man's responsibility?

Actually both should be able to make the decision because both will deal with the consequences of their choice. The choice should be done in faith not in fear with total liberty of conscience. It is important to be able to live in good conscience, the choice will always pause a certain problem for the believers but remember God is merciful and will always be ready to offer forgiveness to the sinners.

Outside marriage the man will leave it to the woman to "bear sole responsibility" so pregnancy will often times be the factor that will separate the couple if they are not married as we live in a society of immediate gratification through pleasures that are not the result of a mature reflexion: that is the price to pay to remove the significance of a stable relationship from sexuality. Both man and woman are equal in the love they engage to give to a child. We must never reduce sexuality to genital pleasures only.

Chapter 17

Catherine: When should a couple take the decision to have or not children?

Before getting engage to be married. This should be discussed when the young couple is starting to talk of the possibility of a future together. Both should reach an agreement of what they would like for their future together. There is the possibility that one of the two does not desire any children in which case more discussion will be needed.

Chapter 18

Marie-Claire: What are the methods that a couple can use to avoid a pregnancy?

The most popular means is to take an oral contraceptive, it prevents the ovulation. There are several types of pills available most of which contain a combination of synthetic estrogenlike and progesteronelike substances. When taken daily for the first 20 or 21 days of the menstrual cycle, these substances apparently prevent the rise of luteinizing hormone that leads to ovulation. Even if ovulation should occur (as it apparently does in some cases), oral contraceptives can still prevent pregnancy in most cases, by thickening and chemically altering the cervical mucus so that it is more hostile to sperm and by making the uterine endometrium less receptive to implantation, but the fact that it makes it harder for the sperm to move toward the uterus it does not make it always impossible and that results into an abortion. For some women the pill has some undesirable side effects, the most serious of which is a tendency to form blood clots, strokes and heart attacks. Of course a smoker should abstain from taking this type of contraceptive. Our Church remains cautious toward this method as it does not necessarily prevent pregnancies from occurring: therefore the famous 97% reliability advertised by the pharmaceutical companies that fabricate them in their laboratories. When you think of conception which is the formation of a zygote and fertilization which is the two gametes uniting to form a zygote are basically two different words meaning pretty much the same thing: a new life coming into existence. When you accept this then you realize that the pill is not a contraceptive but also an abortive tool which raise moral issues.

Sterilization for woman (Tubal Ligation) or man (Vasectomy) is an acceptable mean in certain countries. The tubal ligation consist a surgical sterilization in which the uterine tubes are tied and severed. It prevents the spermatozoa from reaching the ovum to fertilize it and it prevents the ovum from reaching the uterus. While in certain cases it could be reversed once done it is not always the case, most of the time it is irreversible. The vasectomy is also a form of surgical sterilization in which each ductus deferens is tied and cut. It does not interfere with normal ejaculation, but spermatozoa are prevented from entering the semen. That is also irreversible in most cases.

There is also the coitus interruptus that is the withdrawal of the penis just before the male orgasm so that ejaculation does not occur within the female tract. It requires perfect timing by the man. I would not advise it even though the Catholic Church accepts this method because it brings too much insatisfaction, insecurity and anxiety to both man and woman. The reason the Catholic Church accepts this comes most likely from the Holy Scriptures found in Genesis 38:6-10 where it states that Onan by going into his dead brother's wife the child would not be his so he emitted on the ground.

Another way to avoid pregnancy is to abstain from sexual relations during ovulations, some methods consist of detection of ovulation: Several methods of birth control rely on a woman's ability to determine the time of ovulation and to abstain from sexual intercourse for several days preceding and following ovulation. In one method, called the rhythm method, a woman keeps records of the lengths of her menstrual cycles and from these records predicts the length and likely time of ovulation for her current cycle. The rhythm method may be an effective method of birth control if the woman's menstrual cycles are regular and if the period of abstinence from sexual intercourse is long enough. However menstrual cycles can vary in length and the timing of ovulation can vary even when menstrual cycles are regular. Consequently, the likely time of ovulation during a current cycle is difficult to predict with accuracy from records from past cycles.

Another method used to determine the time of ovulation is the measurement of body temperatures. In this method the woman determines her basal body temperature with a thermometer each morning upon awakening and prior to getting out of bed.

Generally a women basal body temperature will be slightly lower prior to ovulation than it will be following ovulation (the higher the temperature following ovulation is the result of rising levels of progesterone).

A third method that fits that group for determining the time of ovulation is the observation of the mucus secretions of the uterine cervix that are discharged at the vagina. Prior to ovulation, estrogens increase the quantity of alkalined cervical mucus that is secreted and they decrease the viscosity and the cellularity of the mucus. These occurrences tend to favor the transport of sperm. Following ovulation, progesterone causes the cervical mucus to become thick. This mucus contributes to the occurrence of conditions that is unfavorable for the penetration and survival of spermatozoa. The vagina, following menstrual bleeding there are several days during which no mucus discharge is present at least nothing that can be seen. These dry days are followed by the onset of mucus that are characterized by the appearance of increasing quantities of cloudy or sticky secretions that can be seen on toilet paper when the woman cleans herself after passing water. Then a few days later can be observed thicker mucus more opaque in substance. Generally, the period from the beginning of the mucus appearance until the fourth day after the last day of appearance of clear lubricative mucus is considered to be a woman's fertile period and with this method the period of menstrual bleeding is also considered as fertile time for the woman. This method is strongly advocated by the Church as it requires the collaboration of the man and the woman and decision must be taken as a couple. It means that the man must show great love and respect for his wife to choose this method is a true demonstration of team work with the two spouses.

There are also condoms and diaphragms; a diaphragm is a thin hemispherical dome of rubber or plastic with a spring margin. It covers the cervix, thereby preventing the entrance of sperm into the uterus. This needs to be fitted in by a physician at first and is generally used in combination with a spermicidal cream or jelly.

The IUD which stands for Intrauterine Device consists of a small spiral, ring, or loop made of plastic, stainless steel or copper and needs to be inserted into the uterine cavity by a physician. Here again you must think this trough because early pregnancy factors have been documented in the presence of IUD users which have caused an abortion to occur. It has caused serious health concerns and even deaths and as a result fewer women use it.

What we call Emergency Contraception Plan has become a more common method of birth control in recent years but it is a misnomer: the result of good marketing propaganda because researches are showing that it acts at times by causing a postfertilization effect regardless of when in the menstrual cycle it is taken; here again the moral implications involved are serious. The side effects are not negligible either: they include thrombophlebitis, lung clots, heart attack, and stroke, and liver damage, development of liver tumors, high blood pressure and kidney disease. Women who smoke are at the greatest risks of developing complications. Ectopic pregnancies have been on the rise with the users of Plan B. What it does is to delay or inhibit the ovulation by altering the endometrium. It can be considered like the contraceptive pill another method to destroy a possibly existing life.

Finally there is induced abortion. It involves using various means to separate the implanted embryo or fetus from the wall of the uterus. The detachment of the embryo or fetus is generally accomplished either by scraping, by saline solutions rinses or by vacuum aspiration (suction).

Now considering the fact that sexual relation are not just the meeting of two bodies, both the meeting of two persons with the full complexity of their psychological make up and with their similar or different cultures we need to look deeper in which method can be acceptable and use by both.

The Catholic Church recognizes that the limitation of birth is part of the responsibility of the married couple for economical and moral reasons. The key recommendations are to treat each other with respect and dignity. While certain methods such as vasectomy and tubal ligation in certain circumstances will be permitted morally it is up to the couple to decide which one is best suit to their needs.

Chapter 19

Gabrielle: What is in vitro fertilization?

When a couple desire to conceive and is unable to after a year or two, many will consult their family doctor who will refer them to fertilization clinics. It is morally wrong because it replaces the natural conjugal union between husband and wife, and often results in the destruction of the embryos. If we are to believe the statistics that show that over 90% of the embryos created in vitro perish at some point in the process that means nine children have loose their lives so that at least one of their siblings may be born. That is sad and so wrong. The Church forbids the donation of eggs and perm and all other form of experimentation of human beings. Until the day when science comes up with something where a fertilized egg in which the chromosomes of the egg and sperm have not been combined to form life such treatments are not recommended. Bear in mind that an embryo has a soul it is not just a piece of material. The Holy Spirit works on the soul of all humans until our death, regardless of our degree of intelligence, success, health or other consideration that humans may have. That is why it is so important to preserve and protect human life.

Chapter 20

Catherine: What if one of the spouses has Aids or another deadly disease what about sex for them?

In certain situations as such I am sure that it would be acceptable to use a condom because we want to protect and preserve life. At this time there are no official guidelines from the Vatican for such cases as they are fairly new happenings. I would simply discuss this with a spiritual guide within the Catholic Church or what ever denomination you choose to belong to. As Christian followers everything should be done with respect of your partner and love.

Chapter 21

Marie-Claire: So where do we go to meet the perfect husband?

I would say that if you do not meet him while in school you will meet him among your circle of friends. I know that you have friends at school, some others with the Air Cadets and you can meet guys by joined clubs such as a photography club or a drama club, you need to find a hobby or something that really interest you where you could volunteer your time in the community and starting there you will get to know people, make friends. Many couples met that way. My mother met her future husband (your grand-father) by making friends in a skating club, eventually her two new friends who were sisters introduced her to their brother. Also never go to bars or night clubs in the hope of meeting Mr. Right, the festive atmosphere and the liquors that are consumed make people appear in a different light, I mean the mood lingering in these places has for effect to hide people's true colors, maybe due to alcohol inhibition but only in part.

The night carries a special atmosphere altogether, I do not know if it has anything to do with the moon and the stars, maybe like the tide movements, the moon also has a gravitational pull on people that affects their brain waves, one thing is sure you see and feel things differently at night than you would under the sunlight! There is a kind of magic floating all around that change your perceptions of things and people. So beware.

It is like meeting people in chat rooms online, they can say what they want and you will never know the difference; maybe it is human nature to try to embellish…You should seek honest relationships and they won't be found in artificial settings.

As for "Love at first sight" it is really a misnomer since love comes from knowledge not from the physical appearance of the person. It could happen to maybe two very lonely people but then again that you only fill a void temporarily once you get to know that person you may encounter deep disappointment. Truly, if you want to meet your future husband join a club that deals with your favorite hobby or learn to play sports or find an organization where you can do volunteer work, there you will meet interesting people. But never forget to pray God to lead you to a good man.

Marie-Claire:

"Hum…I think I just don't know, maybe I will have a career instead of marrying, I will become the best pilot and maybe the first woman to lead a mission into deep space. Maybe I'll go to Europe when I am done with the military and join their Space Agency. And I could have a dog or two to live with me, so I would never be alone. I could live nearby grand-ma Christiane in Belgium. Besides I am not too crazy about children. I don't think I have all that desire for finding the perfect mate."

I am fine with just my friends to surround me. I want money and power!

Gabrielle:

"Me, I would like become an actress; I want to make people laugh to forget about their problems, but if that does not work out I think I would like to be a psychologist for children with problems, because so many have bad parents and as a result have difficulties at school but regardless, I want to get a nice husband, maybe not a good-looking one, so that no one will try to steal him from me but I want him to be funny, to make me laugh. I think there is too much sadness in the world and that people need to laugh. But right now, there are no interesting guys at my school and since I do not like sports so much, I am not meeting anyone that I fancy. It is ok because I am still young and I like to read in peace and visit with my friends.

Catherine:

"I want to get marry in two or three years. I just graduated as a make up artist and if I can establish myself by doing the make up in the fashion world or movie industry or even have my own parfumerie store like the ones I saw in Europe when I went to visit grandma Christiane, I could sell cosmetics and teach at the same time to customers."

OK girls it is getting late, time to go to bed but before turning in for the night just remember this: sex is not a form of social relations. I find it more and more today many teens view sex as nothing else but a way to communicate with another person. I think that it is the result of the family breakdowns that we see around us combined with the easy access to the internet where they have virtual relationships in a virtual world.

The teens feel alienated, alone and abandoned by those who should have been there to guide and protect them. If my parents stop loving each other then there is always a chance that they will stop loving me.That thought would be enough to bring emotional insecurities that in turn translate by giving away what is most precious to us in an attempt to be loved. Now it is really late girls! Go, just go to sleep!

Carol Bellavance

Gabrielle: Mom do you think that aliens really exist; I mean intelligent beings from other planets coming to visit us on earth?

Nice try baby! Go to sleep ~NOW~

About the Author:

I was born and raised in rural Quebec not too far from the border of Vermont. I left when I got married to live in South-Africa; in 1985 I gave birth to our first child Catherine in the small town of Paarl. In 1989 we came back to Canada just in time to give birth to Marie-Claire in Granby, Quebec and when she was three weeks old we moved to Oakville MB, in 1991 Gabrielle saw the day in Winnipeg and soon after that we went to live in Saskatoon SK; from there we moved to Park River ND; where I worked as an emergency medical technician for a while until we moved to Bonsal CA; after a year or so we went to live in Salem OR where I worked for a criminal defense attorney until our return to Canada in 2001. We have lived ever since in the town of Langley in BC; where I graduated as a Medical Office Assistant but went on to work as a Call Center Supervisor. During all those years I have read and reread "Le petit prince" from author Antoine de St-Exupery at least once a year to remind me of what love was about, especially when away from home without any friend that book became my solace.

Printed in Great Britain
by Amazon.co.uk, Ltd.,
Marston Gate.